Trapped Emotions of a Woman

A Book of Poetry

Sonja Lynn Dixon

authorHOUSE®

AuthorHouse™
1663 Liberty Drive
Bloomington, IN 47403
www.authorhouse.com
Phone: 1-800-839-8640

© *2011 Sonja Lynn Dixon. All rights reserved.*

No part of this book may be reproduced, stored in a retrieval system, or transmitted by any means without the written permission of the author.

First published by AuthorHouse 03/24/2011

ISBN: 978-1-4389-5616-9 (sc)

Printed in the United States of America

This book is printed on acid-free paper.

Certain stock imagery © Thinkstock.

Because of the dynamic nature of the Internet, any Web addresses or links contained in this book may have changed since publication and may no longer be valid. The views expressed in this work are solely those of the author and do not necessarily reflect the views of the publisher, and the publisher hereby disclaims any responsibility for them.

Acknowledgments

Praises to my Almighty God who keeps me!

To my loving and beautiful daughters Jasmine, Shermoine, Syna' and Armoni, always be there for one another. Set your goals and accomplish them. Success is measured by what you put out.
Push forward and grow together.

I Love You All

Special thanks to my parents George and Mary Skinner.
To my sister and brother, Eva Skinner and George Skinner Jr.
May God Bless you and I love you.

I have been my worst enemy, constantly telling myself many days and nights no one wants to read what I have written. There were times when I would not write at all because of my fears. Over the years my pen continued to reason with papers, as my heart sung out for help. The longer I went without writing the more it stayed heavy on my mind and bothered me. I placed my fears behind me and decided to move forward with publishing my book. Escaping my pain through writing has inspired me by the many flaws of life. As the ink flows through the pen and out, it represents fallen tears of battered emotions from unhappiness.

If my poetry find its way to you then and only then you will understand what's being expressed. Some of us have been knocked down with words causing emotional pain. Hold your head up high because you have a story to tell as well. I **challenge** my sisters who are experiencing battered emotions, rather it be emotional or physical to branch off from those who will not understand and try to influence you by saying people will know your business, some already do needless to say, you're just left to believe that no one knows. Now, to my sisters who may know of someone or to those who made it out of an situation such as this, don't be afraid to approach another female and say I to have experience that as well and share your story of how you made it. I guarantee you will leave that individual thinking I can make a change. Just think if each one of us did that one thing and touched one soul, how far it will travel and a chain of love travels far beyond than anyone can imagine.

So I say to you if my writing has touched you, think of whom you may help to cross the wall of making a decision that **this can be no more!**

Introduction

The trials I have encountered has inspired me to write this book to share with women from all walks of life whom have experience verbal, emotional, and physical abuse. It doesn't matter if it's from your spouse, partner, or a friend this type of treatment is unacceptable.

I take the time to represent all women who have experience negative thoughts or feelings about themselves from someone who has tried to make them feel less than a human.

As we all know neither experience is better than the other. Because they both leave scars that scorn us for life and sometimes we take it into other relationships, but not intentionally. I look at it like this and so should you; if a man picks constantly at you finding something wrong even when you know there's nothing wrong. My friends the problem is most definitely not you however, it is him as an individual. If he finds the need to pick you apart little by little or uses his hand or fist to show unnecessary affirmative action then he's picking himself apart little by little.

He's simply facing his flaws that needs to be worked out, but somehow not finding the courage to face them. Some men experience verbal or physical abuse if not both as a child while watching a love one close to them suffer. But on the other hand some men use these tactics because it's the only way to feel they have control or the upper hand in a situation. One would think this person would have it compressed in his heart to never treat a woman or any other human being for that matter this way.

Much love to all my sisters from all walks of life

Writing is my passion and my desire
It is who I am
Be within my writing as my writing is within me
To the depths of my soul
Every inch of my body
To every word that flows
For every thought I've had to every thought lost
Writing is my passion
It is my joy of being
It is who I am
Should I fall apart...you will find scrambled words
That has no meaning until I am whole again
I am within my writing as my writing is within me

e·mo·tion (ĭ-mō'shən) n.
1. A mental state that arises spontaneously rather than through conscious effort and is often accompanied by physiological changes; a feeling: *the emotions of joy, sorrow, reverence, hate, and love.*
2. A state of mental agitation or disturbance: *spoke unsteadily in a voice that betrayed his emotion.* See Synonyms at feeling.
3. The part of the consciousness that involves feeling; sensibility: "*The very essence of literature is the war between emotion and intellect*" (Isaac Bashevis Singer).

Dictionary.reference.com

Abuse is only a word, unless put into action. Remove yourself from harmful situations, mental and physical abuse and situations may no longer be harmful to you!

Sonja Lynn Dixon

Contents

Trapped Emotions of a Woman xv

    Branch Over Mine 1
    You Chose Me 2
    Unfelt 3
    Bruised 4
    Alone 5
    Red Tears 6
    Engraved 7
    Tornado 8
    The Bottle 10
    Why I Stop Wearing My Ring 12
    Forgotten 14
    Unspeakable Silence 15
    If I Stayed 16
    Will I Be Blamed 17
    Suppressed 18
    Letting Myself Down 19
    Afraid 20
    You May Not Want To Know 21
    Reflections 23

Part II Trapped Emotions of a Woman 27

    The Power of Crack 28
    "Loving Someone with an Intimacy to Crack" 29
    My Heart Cries 31
    Waking Up To Pieces of Reality 33
    Distant 36
    Broken 38
    KeeZ 39
    It Is You That I Am 40
    I Am To Be 42
    Killing Her Softly 43

You want listen 44
Living Through My Children 46
Born of your Flesh. 48
The Strategies of Life. 49
Situations 51
Resuscitate. 53
Beautiful changes 54
Walking Away. 56
Being Me! 59

Trapped Emotions of a Woman

Trapped Emotions of a Woman — Sonja Lynn Dixon

Branch Over Mine

Will I choose a branch over my sweet and pure apples that has
fallen from my tree

Never!

But if a branch chooses to attach itself to me
it must provide shade from the overbearing sun to care for my fruit

You Chose Me

    you look at me
        and don't like what you see
    who's to blame?
        when you are the one who chose me

Unfelt

He **loves** her
    He loves **her** not
He spends most of his time **not** caring
    She recognizes the feeling of not **being** loved by him
She reaches out to **him** yet he remains distant
    He **continues** to be himself in every way
Spending more time criticizing and not seeing his own **faults**
    She continues **to** reach out to him
Yet **her** touch remains unfelt

Bruised

bruised from words,
i wonder if people see how i feel
bruised from inside out
no one knows what i'm about

bruised from words inside out
like a mother with no breast milk to feed her child
like the naked walking aimlessly waiting to be clothe

bruised from words inside out
feeling, giving of my heart
has caused me to shed tears
wishing all the years spent things were different

bruised from words like...

Alone

Why do I feel alone when I sleep not alone?
Wasted time
Sold memories apart of me,
Has blown my mind.
Taken to a limit that no one knows
Fighting off you, as you pass the blows!

Red Tears

Summer rain
Summer pain
Suits me fine

If it brings happiness from the combustion of being in sane
I'd rather the raining days than to see blood splatter
against the walls
I'd rather deal with the pain of being alone, than to be closed
behind four walls and someone saying lights off!

I'd rather be looking out the window of my room; closed in
prisoner by choice, able to hear the sound of the door opening
by the turn of my own wrist!

We can end the summer rain and summer pain at any time
There is no good or bad time of doing so
Doing it beats the hell out of blood dripping from my
eyes and heart!

Struggling to keep red tears away
Trying to keep it at a bare minimum cost!

Trapped Emotions of a Woman ── *Sonja Lynn Dixon*

Engraved

The pain I wear is engraved in your name
from the stiffness of your love
Wishing the love God gave, you would have shared!

Tornado

My mind revolving like a tornado
Beating against every thought that stands
The ultimate goal is to make it through without
letting the storm tear me down.
Unfulfilled admirations flying
through mid-air, dodging with nothing to hold to
As the strong wind moves me about
I'm pushed against a wall, tampering with a closed door
not knowing what it may hold.
Too weak to bear the storm
My mind revolving like a tornado that beats against every thought!

His I do's turned into I don'ts
　　His I don't said I want
His I will said no need to…
　　His priorities turned into a game of hide and seek
His desire for seeking was at any cost
　　What he did not see in me was who he said I do to!

The Bottle

wanted to hold him
but I reached for you instead
wanted him to fill me within
but it's you who fills me up
i can reach for you with no disappointments
never disappointed of you loosing your taste for me

Trapped Emotions of a Woman ~ Sonja Lynn Dixon

Why I Stop Wearing My Ring

When loving a person you look for the same in return. Most importantly when he has asked for your hand in marriage, there's a fulfillment of joy in the air. Things started out good for us, but as time passed I notice a difference in his attitude. The strangest thing is when you don't have a clue to what caused this reaction. I could never understand what went wrong on my behalf. I like to think of myself as one of the rare breed of women that still exists. The more I thought about it, the crazier I felt. Constantly trying to think of ways to better my marriage. It appeared the harder I tried the more he pushed away, even thinking about it now causes a pain that scuttles through my heart, my soul. Loving someone with no love in return! Now don't get me wrong, as I mentioned earlier he started out being a loving and kind individual, after all I did say I do!

Crazy in my head that he wanted to be alone from me and yet I still wanted him. I can say this; I married into a great family and could have not asked for anything better. I started thinking; I married him for better or for worst what is a girl to do when encountered with so many issues along the way in the early stages of our marriage. I was willing to fight to the end and forget about the past. However, there are few concerns that no matter what I did to forget them; they keep knocking at my heart. Have you ever wonder why one would make decisions that in the long run causes damaged to your family. After a while it was hard giving and not being on the receiving end. It wasn't until then I decided to stop wearing my ring. I stop wearing my ring for love, because I had to accept what was going on and love myself.

I stop wearing my ring for peace. Something he demanded once he walked away, so I found peace within myself. I stop wearing my ring for happiness. To make him happy was to back off and gain peace, and find happiness all over again for my children, myself; after all we still had each other.

Trapped Emotions of a Woman — Sonja Lynn Dixon

Forgotten

    remember the wedding
forgotten love
        communication stopped and felt bitter

    running stream travel
        like tears rolling from my face
searching for some peace and a better place

Unspeakable Silence

just passing through
darkness becomes day
picked a flower from its patch
eyes focusing on the center of its color
to find a resemblances of me underneath
taking me back in time
where there were no worries
only for someone else to have that
as the night passes through
darkness becomes day
my conscience is calling out to me
the sound of darkness is all I hear
silent cries and silent screams
focus on me
blinded by the darkness that seems to be light
my conscience is calling out to me

If I Stayed

If I stay there will be no trust
If I stay I may not give my all as before
If I stay I will not question anything you do
If I stay there is no room for confusion
If I stay you will not have me as before
for I have given my all time and time again.
If I stay you may think there's another
no time for that, have enough to deal with!
My apologies…that I can not stay!

Will I Be Blamed

Will they blame me for not hanging on a bit longer?
Will they understand that I had to do what was needed?

Staying is what I wanted more than anything
But it was the constant reminder and heartache of what I had taken before.

I will stand for what is right even if it cost some to turn against me!

When will we learn to understand the importance of one another?
Should I have understood that some things never change for the better!

Acceptance is the key from beginning to end
As I accept you, the only thing left was for you to accept me!

You did not have to question it
You knew it from the start.

Will they blame me for not hanging on a bit longer!

Suppressed

Dealing with another way to get passed true emotions

My heart revealing what does not need to be known, not even to myself

Ocean of running thoughts turning into scattered pieces

The feeling of a battered individual, only I'm left untouched with trapped emotions, that's just for today

Clutching on to what I had agreed upon

If I continue to suppress the situation, it increases as the moments decreases.

Letting Myself Down

Have I let myself down?
    I apologize for not paying attention to you.

I put others first before myself
    Found no wrong in doing so.

Although I have faced many trials and tribulations
    When others judge, I found no place to.

Feeling my way through the dark
    Realizing there was no answer.

I apologize for not paying attention to you.

Caring for those who did not care back
    My happiness is seeing others happy.

It hurts when others can be so cruel
    At times I felt I had nothing.

Weak I'm not, just misunderstood.

I lost myself some time ago
    I have let myself down.

There were times I wanted to lie down and never get up
    I must bring her back.

I will find my way through the storm.

I apologize for not paying closer attention to you.

Afraid

She's afraid to love again
Afraid of what the next may hold within

Trapped Emotions of a Woman — Sonja Lynn Dixon

You May Not Want To Know

Somebody may not want to know
But it's what we go through
Somebody may not want to know
Can we find another way?

Going through the roller coaster of life
Had I known relationships could cause so much strife

Being mistreated and cheated on
Taking us to heated situations
Misguided conversations

Causing us to feel incomplete with the repeated
verbal and sometime physical abuse
Feeling underachieve

Getting tired and learning to be relieved
Relieved because it took me so long to wake up

Because I gain a little weight
You no longer wanted to participate
You made it known that I disgust you
That's when I reached a breach of not trusting you

Too big to be with you
But not big enough to stimulate you
Sadly mistaken of this situation

You see

Trapped Emotions of a Woman —— Sonja Lynn Dixon

You are the ache in my brain
And now you're wondering who's lame
I have opened my mind to explore where I have not gone before
No longer feeling like the back door
No longer a subject anymore
Because I have opened a new door of finding myself

Watch you stand on the opposite side
While I glide in chanted moments
Relentless days of feeling amaze

Now watch me masturbate
As I stimulate the thought in your head
Wishing it was you instead
Because you were the only one I knew

Nevertheless…

Somebody may not want to know
But it's what we go through
Somebody may not want to know

Reflections

Reflection of me don't turn away
Lift your head in the mirror
So that I may gain a clearer vision of me
A disconnection of selected memories of being taunted
You have let his callous ways take a toll on you
You have tried to make do
Why did you or how did this come about
You see I'm having problems trying to fit everything in its prospective place
So much taken from me in my heart
So much taken away from my soul
I have felt dismayed far too long
If only you had taken the time to conveyed your thoughts
Such a perplex look about yourself
I asked you to get it together
If I look your way or you willing to come back with me
Reach into the reflection of the mirror
You can't erase the obstacle race you have ran
But you can retreat to the down beat to a new rhythm

My heart bleeds for the moment of laughter!

Part II
Trapped Emotions of a Woman

Trapped Emotions of a Woman — Sonja Lynn Dixon

The Power of Crack

A knock at the door
It slowly pushes open
Speechless as I stood
He was asleep in the next room
He appeared to be content and at peace
That was the only time he felt free
Let's say that for the least!
As I stood and watched closely
What was invisible became a visual sight
And this could be seen even if there was no light
It moved slowly down the hall towards the bedroom
Building into what appeared to be a cloud of smoke
at the bedside over him
Watching helplessly with tears rolling down my
face
He did not know, but I knew who she was
She had come for him
She waved her scent back and forward across his face
Still standing my heart began to race
He tossed and turned not sure of what was going on
It was calling for him...or maybe he called out to her
He slowly removed the covers from over him
Reached for his clothing and dressed as though I was
not there
She turned and formed a smile as she moved through
the air like fog
Behind her, there he followed
I called his name but her scent overpowered my voice
Passing by as though he never knew me

He disappeared into the air just as she did
The knock at the door
Is when I realize this can be no more

"Loving Someone with an Intimacy to Crack"

I once loved a man that had an intimacy to crack. When we meet he was very sweet, charming, polite, well mannered and very respectful around my daughters and I. Having a lack of knowledge on crack and the strong hold it has on a person, I was clueless. I never witness the actions being around anyone who suffered from crack. I've seen people on the streets that were on crack, however I did not know there circumstances. I just felt if you have someone to help things could be different for that person, wishful thinking on my part. I was wrong!

I've learn that this drug over powers the mind and the soul of a human being. It destroys the sense of security that an individual once had. It curves the appetite of self motivation to a complete halt and stimulates the mind into thinking this drug "Crack" is all you may need. It totally diminishes a person thinking process and reputation. Crack will lead you into thinking you don't have a problem. It fools a person into thinking this is a habit that can be kicked at any time when in fact it becomes even harder to overcome the more it is use. This drug substance comes between families that make you steal and betray them and any one else to support the habit.

I remembered one night very clearly. He was leaving the house to go with some friends, he looked at me and said I'll be back later, knowing it was payday for him, I called his name and said don't leave! As he turned and looked back at me I no longer saw his face, but the face of the devil smiling at me. Now I know this may sound a little crazy, well maybe a lot but going through challenges like this with someone can make you feel a bit on the unstable side.

He never used the drug in our presence it's the knowing he was on his way to using and the emotional roller coaster I was on.

This addiction can be well hidden by an individual who value their appearance in the public eye. Not all people can be identified if they are using this drug but one drug abuser to another can be identified in an instant. I've seen it done!

Most of us know someone who is struggling with crack. It could be a spouse, child, parent, aunts, uncles or a very close friend. Too many of them will try and even get away with hiding the problem from family and friends which is the wrong thing to do. They are will to go through more problems of hiding their addiction than getting help.

In some cases when family and friends learn of this behavior they become embarrassed and may walk away, nothing to be embarrassed of! Instead of walking away one way of helping a person is by holding a meeting and let that person know in the front of other caring members that they are aware of the problem. It allows that person to either admit or deny their crack addiction and from that point on is where the trouble really begins or the individual will reach out for help. It has to be that person's decision to change and no one else. Accepting the truth and confronting them whether or not they accept it is a big start at least for the family. So many things can be discussed as to the do's and don'ts which is (tough love). Sitting down and discussing this may very well hold your family together in a situation like this.

My advice to a family that's going through this is to never be afraid to face or admit what's going on. As mention before there are many families struggling with the same problem and many go with their backs turned. I believe in my heart we should reach out and help if the help is wanted before letting them go astray. My spouse tried seeking help after being talked to on several occasions or maybe it was the pressure from family that made him seek help. He tried a program which I thought it was working for him. I felt he tried being a new (clean) and a better person looking for a fresh beginning in life, but unfortunately that did not last long at all.

He started the program because he was asked time and time again to get help. No longer afraid of what I had gone through I was willing to share with anyone who was going through the same thing.

He would always apologize for his actions of not being able to pay bills after awhile the shit was tiresome hearing the same thing over again. I went from raising all kind of hell to just looking at him when he entered the bedroom from his crack binges. I think that bothered him the most, me keeping quiet and saying only one day you will get tired. As time went on and a couple of years passed I decided to move on with life. It was the best thing I could have done for me and my daughters.

It is better to love with tough love than to love with empathy for it only rottens the situation.

My Heart Cries

My heart cries out to what you have put me through
Telling myself one day soon there will be no more tears falling from this face
No more frowns of sorrow leaving a trace
But days filled with tears of joy and laughter will shine everlasting

No more time for foolishness in my life
Problems, pain and broken hearted
For life itself has much more to offer

Tell me,
Was it worth it?
The time and effort you put forward
Would you do it again?

Breathless I am
You have caused me to feel the need to be alone

Why!
When I have done no wrong
Only by pleasing you
Wasn't I good enough

You turned your back on me
Problems, pain and broken hearted

We decided to give it another try
Then you introduce *IT* to me all over again

Go,
For it is God who can redeem my soul

I will pave a new road to travel because of you
And
Because of you I will be untouchable

Waking Up To Pieces of Reality

Lying in my bed sound asleep
Having a bad dream and many things
Waking from a dream as if I had bitten
into someone
The taste of blood in my mouth
Feeling pieces of bones lie on my tongue
Spirits flying through the air of my bedroom
As I awake from my sleep
What I thought was a dream became reality
Back and forward across the ceiling
No faces seen just form of different sizes flying
in the air
Looking down at me with silent loud sounds only
I could hear
After sitting up and realizing what was going on
I was under attack

My room wasn't hot or cold, just a feeling I can't
quite explain
The presence of spirits were definitely real
I felt afraid but not overwhelmed with fear, because
I knew of a higher power
I started praying and asked God to step in and take
control
I then picked up my phone and called a friend
After explaining what was going on she immediately
began to pray
I laid down waiting to see the next day
No idea that I would not wake up to a bad dream and
many things

Trapped Emotions of a Woman — *Sonja Lynn Dixon*

Blood was no longer dripping from my mouth
Pieces of bones no longer lay on my tongue
Spirits no longer flew from wall to wall
Waking up to a bad dream and many things
One thing left behind was the taste of blood in my mouth
Even then I exhale after waking up to pieces of reality

Trapped Emotions of a Woman — Sonja Lynn Dixon

Grasping for lost time that can't be replaced bring back the time lost so that I can start over again!

Distant

Emotional from the burning flames of yours words
Distant far beyond I can see
Distant till there is no unknown
Folding my arms like an angry child
Bottling my thoughts
Distant in my soul
Distant in my mind
Distant are my thoughts
Keeping them from being exposed
Selling my soul
Only by being with you
Feels like I'm burning in hell
My soul
My mind
Can't see
My thoughts
My arms no longer exist
As my skin turns to ashes
My legs I can't feel not having the strength
to walk away
Distant is my soul
Distant is my mind
Distant are my thoughts
Tormented in flames
Save me from what's killing me

Trapped Emotions of a Woman ~~~ Sonja Lynn Dixon

Soul
Mind
Thoughts
Save me so I can feel me again
To feel and believe that my soul exists
To feel and believe as I once did
To know that I can think again
To know my thoughts are no longer thoughtless thoughts
Save me, so I can feel me again!

Broken

many words unspoken
their bond has been broken
between man and woman

no longer friends
but share a love child

never in my wildest dreams
would I ever imagine this could be?

their bond has been broken
between man and woman

he pretends to not know her
yet he sees a part of her

he is furious of the changes
not understanding she had been protecting him

their bond has been broken
between man and woman

she puts the anguish in the past were it belongs

yet his anger still seems to stand strong

a bond broken
between man and woman.

KeeZ

Autumn comes and goes
We have seen and not seen
Years passed us by and the presence of you is like spring time
My cloudy mind is no longer cloudy
This old heart is changing colors
Blooming into something beautiful
Sharing sentimental thoughts back in time
How I wish all my good times and bad could have been shared with you
A constant reminder of the sweetness of your lips
The gentleness of your hugs
I remember passing you by not enough courage to say
I remember you left for a while and even then seeing you my feelings were the same…
My lips shut tight still not enough courage to say…
Do you think it's too late now?
Too late for us to give it a try
You have treated me with such kindness
Never raising your voice at me
Same soft gentle tone then and now
For you to come back my way
Life is offering us another chance to show one another what real happiness can be
Now I can only wonder where I would be without you

It Is You That I Am

Lost in my own sorrow
Lost in my dreams
How I wish this was an illusion
Destined to be free
I look like her but act like you
Not here for me and never bother to be
I don't know your likes and dislikes
Gasping for the same air that you breathe
I often wonder are there others like me
One who looks, walk, and act as I do
Receiving no love from you while it was
very much needed

I remember your face
I remember your complexion
Never realizing the one I'm born from was
darker than me
It is you the same complexion I am
What else do we share?
Why did you abandon me?
Was I not what you wanted?
Did you not ask for me?
You left a mark on me

Trapped Emotions of a Woman — Sonja Lynn Dixon

But this I'll try and save my children from
It is you the same complexion I am
My heart suffering in tears trying to understand why
Did your thoughts not change once you laid eyes upon me?
My thoughts will remain the same as they are
It is you the same complexion I am

I Am To Be

I am to be eternal
Set free from contradicting stories and lost allies
Moving in space
As though I'm in a race
Keeping my cool from getting a case

I am to be
Moving in time with no speculations
Trying to remember where I spent my last dime
Gaining energy as I go
Never settling to the same flow
As my mind get lost in space
A sweet silhouette sits across my face
I am to be

I Am To Be

Killing Her Softly

He's standing on the street corner watching women as they pass him by. Believing to be the greatest of them all. He tries to capture their attention. He sees one from a distance and she became his prey. From the hard and intense stare, causes her to stumble. Her clothes are ripped into pieces, leaving them not fit to cover her body again. After undressing her, he then pulls himself up with blood dripping across her thighs. People passing by and no one offered to help. Once he took his eyes off of her she was able to grab hold to a pole and pull herself up. He walks back to the corner as if nothing happened waiting and watching for his next victim. She stood tugging and fixing on her skirt, still unable to focus and grasp what just happened as people continued to pass her by. No one bothered simply because he rapped her with his eyes.

You want listen

Lost child that no one hears,
dealt with the long harsh years
he sheds no tears, visible as we can
see.
.

His ways no more than the average teen boy
inherited ways from both ends
let him make way and explore as they all do
discipline is one thing, but taking away is another.

Trapped with no place to go
in fear of hurting one soul.

You may be better off in other places
before you stumble and fall over your loose
shoelaces.
Feeling your way through as a child, growing
into a man, walking on pieces of broken vases.

I have tried to embrace you with encouraging
words of wisdom and love.
Don't want to replace her, just help you erase
the anger and pain that is stored away.

Trapped Emotions of a Woman ∼ *Sonja Lynn Dixon*

Spoke words to you to pray above, because I
know you're tired of...
One day your soul will be free like a beautiful
dove.

Hope this doesn't rub of on you the wrong way
for I know there's a sweet and gentleness about you
stay strong, because God has his hands on you.
What do you think of when you sit alone in quiet
places?
Do the memories you hate the most run races
between the different faces you try to carry?

God sees, hears, and know of your pain
and from this you will gain.

ADK

Living Through My Children

I have the opportunity to relive again
To do what I was told
To do what I should have done
To do what I did not do

Tell me…is this wrong

Living through my children
I will not make them do what I miss doing
But I will push them to do what is needed
I will conquer all great things through them

I feel God has bless me to get it right this time
Not once, but four times
I will guide them
Talk to them
Show them
Push them
Take them
Drive them
Guard them when I can

Tell me…is this wrong

If giving them the push to do better than me
Then I will be wrong
If pushing them to get a college degree is
wrong
Then I will be wrong
If telling them to guard their credit is wrong
Then I will be wrong
If telling them to strive for the best they can
be is wrong
Then I will be wrong

Trapped Emotions of a Woman — Sonja Lynn Dixon

If having them to stay home until college is completed is wrong

Then I will be wrong

If advising them not to judge others is wrong
Then I will be wrong
If explaining the do's and don'ts on how a woman should be treated is wrong
Then I will be wrong
If telling them a teenage boy is not what's important is wrong
Then I will be wrong
If teaching them to cook and clean and not to count on others is wrong
Then I will be wrong
If telling them education is first, an excellent paying job, marriage and then children is wrong
Then I will be wrong

If explaining to them the mistakes I have made is wrong
Then I will be wrong
If telling them to pick yourself up and continue through life because one mistake will not be the last you make is wrong
Then I will be wrong

If sharing these things with four gifts from God is wrong
Then guess what,
I will be wrong

For everything I started and did not complete
For everything I thought about doing and did not
I believe they will accomplish and be better

Tell me…
Is Living Through My Children Wrong

Trapped Emotions of a Woman ⁓ Sonja Lynn Dixon

Born of your Flesh

You stayed around long enough to fertilize the soil
But not long enough to watch your roots grow
Here with me
Born of your flesh

Not long enough to watch how tall they would grow
Not long enough to stand beside them as they may fall
Born of your flesh

Did not bother to come back around to see how your roots has blossomed into something beautiful
Here with me
Born of your flesh

None existence you are
Marked yourself as a reminder

For what!

Only to have claim
To what is non-existence to you?

Gravity has it's time

Look around
What you created lasted due to me
The creator to whom you have no knowledge of
Born of your flesh

Yet you sit around claiming
Because you marked yourself as a reminder
Here with me
Born of your flesh

The Strategies of Life

Do I push or just walk away
No one seems to notice the hard effort and work that I put in
Do I push or just walk away

Getting the job done in a timely matter to please all
To find that my work is done in vain
Do I push or just walk away

Asking questions to better myself, so that I may be able to step in
at any given time
Very knowledgeable of what I know, yet driven and they don't know
Do they even care that I struggle from paycheck to paycheck, hell I might
not have a bite to eat and yet make way for my children to eat
Has justice prevail, when it feels like its raining hail.
I sit and nod my head am I none existing, do they not put the paper in
my hand directly or does it sit there and before the day is up the work is
magically done
Do I push or just walk away

Too much underhanded shit going on, but who will take a stand for what's
going on
If I grumble loud enough my job may end, if I sit and continue nodding
then they will never know
Do I push or just walk away

Who in the hell has the right to say not you, but we will give it to you.
My light skin complexion does not help me no more than an incarcerated
black man
Do I push or just walk away

I'm so damn tired of trying and trying and trying

Guess I better take a stand for myself, who in the hell will if I don't

Trapped Emotions of a Woman — Sonja Lynn Dixon

So I guess I may be unemployed, oh well if they can't handle a sister telling them like it is
After all I'm the same damn paper pushing sister that gets their work out in a timely matter, only for the higher paid to continue getting paid more and the underpaid still go underpaid, stressed, more work and oh yeah we will give you a 3% percent raised
But you have to do this, this and this
Now if you please sign your name on the dotted line
Do I push or just walk away

Gotta keep a smile on my face and don't show the disgrace on the inside as my throat
flutters with frustration
Because someone might be standing their laughing on the inside that I did not get it because…
They know damn well they did not stand a chance
Do I push or just walk way

Don't want to keep pushing, to only find myself up against a rubber wall
Don't want to walk away because it may cause me to stumble and fall
Do I push or just walk away

Situations

Situations rising beneath my breast
As though I'm in quicksand
Waiting for you to come and rescue me
The image of you is clearer as the situations
    deepens

As my thighs tightens to the sound of unwanted
    words
Slowly sinking, waiting for you to rescue me
My arms extended reaching for the blue skies
Why oh why!
Why are you not here as my thighs tighten from
    exhaustion?

Your smile I see marked in the white clouds
Your touch I feel for the last time
With my arms still extended to the skies
Cries of why?

With welcoming arms I walk in
And you say...My child do not fear
As I stand with a gleam behind me
He reaches out and just from a touch I felt the
    motion of his love, moving from him to me

As situations rise beneath my breast
There is still time
Do not be afraid, for I am who you once knew
Prepare as I set you free to try again
I'm told that I am strong

Trapped Emotions of a Woman — Sonja Lynn Dixon

Most of the time I want to be left alone
Keeping myself from going under
Mixed up from many thoughts in my head
What if this
What if that
Why can't things just be?
I'm told that I am strong
Please just leave me alone!

Resuscitate

I died three times in my sleep, and God resuscitated me
My body jumped and lifted from the bed and settled back in place
I laid there with my eyes open looking around and not moving
God resuscitated me.

Thirty minutes later my body was given life again

Another thirty minutes later, God resuscitated me again
My body jumped!
As I laid there lying still, nothing but my eyes moving about.
I searched the ceiling for answers as I laid still in the darkness of my room.

He gave me life again
He placed my soul back in me
I closed my eyes not knowing of his will.

Was God using my body, my life, my soul to breathe life in another?
Was God breathing life back into me?
God resuscitated me!

Beautiful changes

will I look the same as life, season changes
The weekend measuring with sweet sounds of love and laughter
    wrapped with nice sensible songs to a desire taste

Peacefully watching
    sitting with a stern boldness as my eyes set in

Calm evenings of love and laughter with someone you love
    always warm the soles

Trapped Emotions of a Woman ～ *Sonja Lynn Dixon*

Seeing you puts a smile on my face
Wishing I could feel your warm embrace
No longer afraid,
Because you are my first aid!

Trapped Emotions of a Woman — *Sonja Lynn Dixon*

Walking Away

Seeing you puts a smile on my face
Wishing I can feel your warm embrace
You have no idea what you mean to me

No longer afraid
Because you are my first aid

When I saw you walk away
I wonder if there will be another day
For me to stare into your eyes again

Seeing your smile play over and over
in my head is crazy
Sitting still, thinking, capturing the moment
This feeling makes me lazy
Not wanting to move afraid of loosing
the vision of your beautiful face

So please, please...

I feel free now
Like I'm wearing a crown
Lifted a big burden of letting you know
I have been running
Keep in mind you are my number one

So please, please...

I will protect your heart
And remember this from that start

I have love you since the day I laid eyes on you
And this is true
We have encountered a problem keeping us apart

Trapped Emotions of a Woman ——— *Sonja Lynn Dixon*

But know that I'm not far
I love the color of your skin
I love how you let me in
I love how you step inside my mind
Loving you is like tasting the finest wine

You are the man I have wanted but could never have
Sitting here bring tears to my eyes
Just knowing your presence is someone near
I know longer fear

My mind may reflect back
my heart is going through a healing process
a journey travel to which I will never return
join me
want you,
come
peace
awaits you!

Being Me!

I am a woman indeed
One that has not met much of her needs
I have went through life pleasing others
For me, not much covered
    I cry tears of pain of not knowing me
Going through life all this time pleasing others and not myself
What was I thinking, because I'm left alone to fill my way through
No help with this one
Satisfaction to me was pleasing others and seeing them happy,
But what about me.
I forgot about myself and even at the tender age of 39, I feel left out.
I know what I like and what I don't like, but what about me
What's really inside of me?
Am I holding tight to something that even I can't reveal?
Am I afraid of just being me, Afraid that I may let someone down
Afraid to say the wrong thing, Afraid …afraid

Trapped Emotions of a Woman — Sonja Lynn Dixon

My pen and pad may cause trouble, but I be damned if I take a triple dose of what I have been dealt!

LaVergne, TN USA
01 April 2011

222420LV00003B/10/P